Blogger Mentoring & SEO Strategies

By J.M. Troppello
Publisher of Mustard Seed Sentinel

A Word from the Author

This book is meant to be a guide that can help you learn better blogging and SEO techniques. All tips and strategies shared in this guide are not a guarantee that your website or blog online ranking will automatically increase. However, if you invest the requisite time and energy into this blogger mentoring and SEO strategies guide, you may increase the probability of succeeding as a blogger online. All results from this guide may vary. No two results will be the same. By reading and applying this course, you assume responsibility for your actions as an active participant to thoroughly read through this guide and effectively apply the tips and techniques to your own website or blog.

- J.M. Troppello
Publisher of Mustard Seed Sentinel and owner of Mustard Seed Marketing Group, LLC

Table of Contents

Chapter One

How to Write Copy That Meets Google's Content Quality Guidelines

If you want to take your blog to the next level and improve your site's online ranking, you need to have a good understanding of the quality guidelines which Google uses to rank content on the Internet. If you have the time, you can read through the 164-page Google Search Quality Guidelines. However, it's likely you are too busy, so you can read this chapter to learn some tips on how to meet their content quality guidelines.

You must improve your search engine optimization (SEO) copywriting skills to give your blog content more of a chance to succeed and be read by a bigger audience. The first step is to understand what Google is looking for when ranking content online.

Learn How to Meet Google's Content Guidelines with These Tips

Global content "raters" are contracted by Google to identify the value of content as it relates to the parameters established in their PDF guide. When you write blog and website content that meets these guidelines, that improves the chances of your work being found in search engine results pages (SERP).

- **Write High-Value Content.** Clearly defined content that adds value to the reader will rank higher in Google searches. You need to write blog content that is more valuable than your competitor's blogs so that your site ranks higher in SERP. Remember that raters are checking to see how your content meets the PDF guidelines.
- **Create Expert Content.** The standards for quality content are high in the Google PDF. Learn as much as you can about the topic you're writing about for each blog post. Become an expert. Write content that will get picked up by other websites and linked to as a backlink—to increase your chances of ranking higher.
- **Use a Conversational Tone.** Gone are the days when you needed to write in a long-winded manner, sharing as much knowledge as possible. You still need to provide high-quality value to your readers. However, use a conversational

tone. Google raters place a higher value on high-quality content that is written in a conversational tone. The modern reader has a lower attention span. Use a header and sub-headers, shorter paragraphs, and bullet points or numbered lists. This improves conversion rate optimization (CRO).

- **Improve PQ Rating.** You need to place a high value on writing error-free content, but it must also engage the reader. Your content will receive a higher page quality (PQ) rating when you write dynamic content that meets the reader's search request needs.
- **Review Niche Guidelines.** When writing niche content, you are required to meet a higher level of standards if you want your work to rank better. For example, "Your Money or Your Life" (YMYL) pages which provide content on finances or lifestyle advice must be written by an expert or with expertise—to rank higher in SERP. Usually this content shares financial tips, legal advice, news, or nutritional information which can impact a reader. It's regulated more intensely by Google raters due to this impact. Google wants to rank high-value, quality content higher.
- **Write Trustworthy Content.** These global rates review online content to ensure that it comes from a trustworthy source that meets Google's guidelines for Expertise, Authoritativeness, and Trustworthiness (EAT). One example is that medical websites that provide content from accredited medical experts will rank higher in SERP.

Write Blogs with a Purpose

Sure, you want to write blogs that share your message, but if you want to be found by more readers, you need to write optimized content. If not, then you are wasting your time and you won't expand your readership base as quickly as if you followed the Google content guidelines.

Don't become a slave to SEO and lose your own unique personality and writing tone. However, find a way to effectively mesh these two factors to create the best high-value content that will get seen by more readers—as your blog climbs its way to page one on SERP.

Are You Ready to Create High-Quality Blogs?

Get started on your action plan today to write more quality content for your blog or website. Show a level of expertise with a conversational tone that truly engages the readers. Improve your PQ rating and work diligently toward meeting the expertise requirements for niche content writing. Get started today by learning the tips outlined in this blogger mentoring book so you can take the online world by storm and make your mark as a top-ranking blogger!

Chapter Two

Use These SEO Techniques to Improve Blog Ranking

Maybe you're a new blogger and everything about SEO seems extremely overwhelming. You may have been blogging for a long time and feel like giving up because you haven't been able to increase your readership base.

However, SEO for blogging doesn't have to be overwhelming.

Writing blogs that rank high in SERP involves more than just creating error-free content that quickly engages the reader.

Start the journey toward getting more visitors to your blog by implementing the following five basic SEO techniques. You can create optimized blog content that will get better results.

ncrease Blog Ranking with These SEO Tips

. Use Keywords as Naturally as Possible

ears ago, SEO involved stuffing keywords, but that created stilted content that nade little sense to readers and added less value to their search needs. Google's lgorithms have changed and now keyword stuffing is not good. Your content can be enalized by Google—with a lower ranking—if you stuff keywords.

Make all of your hard work count. Use a natural conversational tone in your writing hat works well with the fast-paced mentality of today's blog readers. Remember, hat Google places a higher value on a superior user experience (UX) than a bad one. Keyword stuffing creates a bad UX.

Create a better UX by integrating the keywords in a naturally flowing conversational one. When readers are happy, they will come back for more of your content. Repeat raffic to your site means it will rank higher in SERP.

2. Place a High Value on Optimized Content

Google penalizes websites which do not provide high-quality content to readers. Improve the possibility of a higher ranking, by only publishing high-quality blogs and website content.

Get to know your audience so you have an easier time of ascertaining what type of content they want to read. You can use survey forms or email surveys to your subscriber list to find out which blogs they like and which ones they don't. This can help you in creating relevant content for your target audience that will continue to cultivate a loyal readership base.

Use shorter two to four sentence paragraphs, as well as headers, sub-headers, and bullet points or numbered lists to make the reading experience more reader friendly.

3. Create Optimized Title Tags

Your content will appear on Search Engine Results Pages (SERP). So, it's extremely important to create optimized title tags. This is the first impression a reader will get of your content while they are performing online searches.

Craft headlines which include the relevant keyword to ensure simplified crawling of the content by Google bots. This can also make your content more visible to potential readers searching online.

Titles longer than 70 characters will be cut by Google in the SERP. Don't stuff too many keywords in the title. Focus on the main keyword. Make sure you include the keyword toward the beginning of the title since only 70 characters are included online.

Quickly engage the reader and improve the click-through-rate (CTR) of your blog by writing a dynamic title. According to Moz.com, titles with the most dynamic sounding headlines had an increased (CTR). Write a headline which includes a Top Ten List or something that is going to make today's blog readers *need* to click through and read the content.

4. Don't Forget About LSI Keywords

If you are a beginner blogger, you may not be familiar with Latent Semantic Indexing (LSI) keywords. Basically, LSI keywords relate back to your main keyword.

You can use an online tool like Latent Semantic Indexing to enter ten "seed keywords" and then LSI keywords are generated for you.

For example, you might be writing a blog about "blogger mentoring." You can use LSI keywords like "blog techniques," "blogger tips," and "blogger advice." When you use LSI keywords, you are giving Google the chance to fully identify the overall purpose of your blog content or website copy.

5. Integrate Content with Authority

You can increase the ranking of your blog content by integrating authoritative information such as statistics, expert statements, infographics, and other pertinent content depicting your authority on the subject. Even if you are not an authority on the content, providing this authoritative information adds to the relevance of your overall material. Remember to include content that has a high domain authority.

You can use the Alex Rank app for android or iOS or use the Alexa Rank extension for Chrome to check the ranking of your blog, website, or any website—like a competitor's site. I have also started using the SEMRush toolbar extension for this purpose. They have both free and paid services. These tools can be used to help you find high ranking domains from which to gain authoritative information for research for your own content. Remember this is for research purposes only. Don't plagiarize and always be sure to site sources in your articles.

Use keywords as naturally as possible. Place a high value on optimized content. Create optimized title tags. Don't forget to use LSI keywords. Integrate content that has authority and will rank higher.

Chapter Three

Use These Tips to Write Superior Online Copy

Content plays a vital role in making sure that your blog or website ranks higher in search engines. When writing articles, blogs, or landing pages for your website, the word length needs to cover a wider context base instead of shorter copy.

How to Write Superior Online Content

You will begin to organically increase your SERP ranking when you start to become smarter in your copywriting efforts. Read through the following copywriting tips and consider implementing them into your online blogging strategy.

1. **Content length** is a main factor included in Google's algorithm which ranks websites. Write superior quality content for each blog and website page so you increase the possibility of getting a higher SERP.

Online content such as blog posts and website pages which have higher word counts such as over 1000 words tend to rank higher. However, it is important to avoid boring your readers. Bored readers quickly leave the site, increasing your bounce rate. That's bad for your ranking. You want readers to stay on your site for as long as possible. Provide relevant information that is reader friendly.

2. Start **targeting personalized online searches** by getting localized with your content. Local searches are getting more popular today. Many internet searches are completed by individuals searching for restaurants, shops, and other places with "near me" in their keywords.

Some personalization factors to consider for people searching online include their current location, language, and their browsing history. All content published on the internet should always provide relevant information that is helpful to users and answers their online searches. Unless you want to remain totally private, like most bloggers do—you should provide some form of contact information such as an address, if your website represents a business. **This is not as relevant for bloggers, writers, and authors**.

However, it is important to note that you shouldn't overly saturate your content with localized keywords. Oversaturation of localized keywords will negatively impact your Google ranking.

3. **Mobile-friendly content** is important in improving your online ranking. Mobile devices are being used more often by people to check websites and read blog posts. If your site is not optimized for mobile viewing, readers will leave. That could negatively impact your online ranking.

4. Before you start writing a blog post, **think of the keywords** you want to rank for online. You need to have a strategy in place and not leave it to chance. There needs to be a method to your madness—not just some haphazard word vomit on the page.

It is important to place the keywords in the following areas:

- Title or main heading
- Any subheaders
- In the 1st paragraph
- Naturally in the content
- In the meta description

Just remember never to oversaturate the content with the keywords. Your content must be readable otherwise readers will leave. Google is all about the readers who search online. They want to make their user experience (UX) great. That's why if your blog or website doesn't provide a superior UX, it won't rank as high.

5. Don't get too focused on SEO. Sure, that's very important. However, you don't want to lose your edge as a creative writer. Remember, Google places **high value on creativity and original content**.

Today's online reader is oversaturated with content. Find a way to stand out, while following Google's quality content standards so your site ranks higher and gets viewed by new readers.

Write content that ranks well with the updated Google algorithm. Craft detailed content that doesn't overwhelm the reader. When it pertains to you, write localized content for those personalized "near me" searches. Make your site mobile friendly. Find the right balance with integrated keywords. Focus on one or two keywords and long tail keywords in approximately 20 percent of the overall content.

Chapter Four

Use These Content Creating Idea Apps

The system of mobile apps started in 2008. In the last ten years, millions of apps have been created. There are approximately 6 million apps available on Google Play, in the Amazon AppStore, and in the iOS App Store. One example is the app Headspace that was designed to augment our concentration levels—which is sorely needed these days since we're inundated with content and losing our longer attention spans by spending too much time on social media.

When you write a blog post, you want to provide content to your readers and usually include a call-to-action (CTA), which you hope readers respond to.

However, sometimes you may be staring at your blank laptop screen and nothing is coming to mind. You've got no keywords or topic to write about. You're experiencing writer's block.

Don't let that blank screen dull your senses any longer. Take a look at these content creating apps that just might be the answer in inspiring your next blog post.

Five Great Content Creating Apps

1. The **Creativity** app can help you brainstorm ideas for your next blog. It was designed to generate ideas from a variety of viewpoints. You can use some of the app features such as Random Words, Six Thinking Hats, and Write Text.

The basic version is free, but it has some limitations. You can upgrade to the Pro version for access to more features. The app is available for Android through the Google Play Store.

2. Ernest Hemingway was known for impacting the reader by writing short sentences. The **Hemingway App** was designed to help the user create bolder and more concise writing, by eliminating long sentences. Remember, today's readers value shorter paragraphs and easy to read content—and so does the Google algorithm.

You can use the app to copy and paste your text in the app platform. The app then evaluates ways you can shorten sentences to improve readability.

3. The Blogging 101 app was designed to provide simple tutorials on how to write blogs and generate content that increases ranking and converts leads. You can use the tools and resources on this app to help you write relevant, reader-friendly, dynamic blog posts.

The app was designed to generate blog topics that are more likely to get clicks. Additionally, this app platform enables easy integration of SEO tips into your blog content.

4. If you need more help thinking of blog topics, use the BRNSTRM Idea Generator. You can generate ideas, topics, and titles for your blogs. The platform is easy to navigate. New categories for content creation are continually being added by the app creators. You will never again be stuck trying to think up topics for your next blog post.

5. Today's busy readers want to stay current on news and trends. The Feedly app can inspire your next blog post since it was designed to keep track of news stories from various online sources. You can get notified about real-time news alerts which may inspire your next post.

Writers and bloggers need help sometimes to continually create relevant blog posts. Use some of these apps to spice up your blog writing routine.

Chapter Five

How to Wisely Use the 280 Characters on a Tweet on Twitter

Have you been struggling with promoting your blog on Twitter? If so, then this chapter is written specifically for you.

In the last two years, Twitter has seen significant growth with an increase of 6 million new monthly users. That is a high number of new users for the Twitter platform.

Make the most of every tweet. You only get 280 characters per tweet. Check out these steps on how to improve your engagement and promotion strategy on Twitter.

Use these Steps to Create Dynamic Tweets

Did you know that there are approximately 336 million active Twitter users each month. That's a lot of people. It can seem overwhelming when you're trying to make your mark and get a tweet to go viral.

1. Play Nicely When You're in the Twitter Sandbox

Make your interactions on Twitter conversational in tone. Don't sound robotic. Speak your mind but steer clear of insulting other users or being offensive. Remember, you want to gain followers, not lose them.

If people start trolling you, don't engage. You can simply block their profile from being able to see your tweets and they can't contact you. You can mute conversations or tweets. You have control of your Twitter experience. Be nice and most people will reciprocate.

2. Follow the 80/20 Rule

If you promote your blog posts all day long on Twitter, you are not going to increase your following. People see that as spam and don't want any part of that.

Follow the 80/20 Rule. You should engage with followers and other accounts 80 percent of the time. Only promote your blog or other links 20 percent of the time. This may seem counterintuitive when you're trying to promote your blog, but it isn't.

Most of the people on Twitter want to engage with others. They're not on this social media platform to promote anything. You need to cultivate "relationships" with people on social media so that they come to respect you. Soon enough, you'll be gaining new followers and will make connections with other bloggers—which can help with networking.

Twitter is more fast-paced, unlike Facebook. You can tweet more often than post on Facebook. Tweet several times a day—like up to 30 times—but make sure you are retweeting others in your network. Then they will start retweeting your content.

I've been on Twitter since 2010. I used to automate my content and following through TweetAdder. Last year, Twitter said automation was no longer allowed. Once I started applying these principles six months ago, my following grew from 2,500 to 13,400. What I'm writing here really works. Engagement is better than promotion.

3. Stay Connected to Your Followers

Stay relevant with current events. Tweet about things that matter to you and your followers. When you tweet relevant content, that increases the chance of engagement with followers.

Check out the National Day Calendar to find relevant days that you can tweet about. For example, October 14th is National Dessert Day. If you like desserts, you can tweet about your favorite on that day.

Stay relevant with your followers by using hashtags. Remember that the life of a tweet is very short, only seconds. Unless it gets replied to or retweeted. Using hashtags can bring new life to the tweet.

When you use the right hashtags, that can increase the impressions—or views—of the tweet. You can see trending hashtags each day to see if you're interested in tweeting about any of them.

Third-party applications like RiteTag, Sprout Social, and Trendsmap can give you a more in-depth view of trending hashtags.

4. Write Compelling Tweets

You want your tweets to add value to your follower's lives. You can do that by showing your unique personality. If you see life as a glass half-full type of person, share positive and inspirational content. If you're more sarcastic and enjoy getting a laugh, write witty tweets.

Compel people to follow you because you are providing content that has a purpose and means something. Follow magazine accounts that interest you and retweet informative articles. Comment on the retweet with a short explanation of why you liked the article.

Tweet helpful information like apps for writers or bloggers that you have used. Foster goodwill among you, your followers, and the network of bloggers you're developing.

5. Tweet Only After You've Thought It Through

Sure, some people tweet whatever comes to mind, without thought to the consequences. However, if you are a blogger who wants to build a respectable reputation, you need to think before you tweet.

You don't want some rash reply to come from you in response to a negative comment by someone. With the current social and political climate, you're likely to get blocked and/or reported by someone. That can possibly get your account suspended temporarily or permanently.

Now, that may not be the end of the world for some people using Twitter. However, if you're trying to build a following on Twitter to increase your blog readership, you need to play by the rules, be a thoughtful tweeter, and respect other people.

If all else fails, start an account on Parler or Minds.com. They don't censor people—especially conservatives—like Twitter and Facebook and other social media platforms have done. I started an account on Parler and Minds, in case I ever get permanently suspended from Twitter.

Chapter Six

Use These Five Writing Tools to Write Better Social Media Posts

Writing content for use on social media platforms is different than writing blog posts. One obvious difference is the word count and the audience attention span. Reading a blog post takes more patience for a reader to get through than a smaller tweet on Twitter, or post on Facebook or Instagram.

You can write better social media posts by using the following five writing tools. They can help elevate your content and improve reader engagement on social media.

Take the Social Media World by Storm with These Writing Tools

Error Free Content is just as important in a social media posts as in a blog post. Every time you write content online, you should proofread before publishing. Remember, that you are trying to build your reputation as a professional blogger.

You can use the Slick Write tool to make sure your content is error free. With this tool, it's easy to copy and paste your social media content into the platform to check for misspellings or grammatical errors before posting on social media. This will take extra time. However, if you're prone to making errors when posting on social media, you should consider using this tool.

Writing Tweet Threads. Most of the time, you won't write tweet threads, but there may be times when this is important—especially if you have something vital to write which amounts to more than the 280-character count.

You can create great tweetstorm threads using the Writerack tool. These threads can significantly impact your followers and can possibly increase your following. With this tool, you can automate any important tweet threads, so you don't have to input each one manually. Just don't do too many threads and annoy followers.

Always Avoid Plagiarism. Plagiarism is bad. There is no excuse for it. Most writers and bloggers have no issue avoiding plagiarizing when they write blog posts or articles. However, when writing social media posts, this can sometimes become a problem. It could be easier to plagiarize than you realize.

Using the Help.PlagTracker online tool can help to make sure your social media content is original. You may not even realize it, but you could have accidentally plagiarized someone else's online social media content. You are building your brand as a professional blogger and always want to deliver original content that showcases your unique voice.

Simplified Content Works Best. Simple is better when posting on social media. You need to be concise and avoid wordiness when writing for Twitter, Facebook, LinkedIn, and Instagram.

We're circling back to the Hemingway App because this tool is ideal for helping you cut content that is too wordy. You can easily revise any content that contains too many adverbs or an overuse of passive voice.

Consistently Proofread Online. This tool is geared toward users who don't have the time to review all their social media content and they need to outsource proofreading. It's mentioned here in this chapter as an option for those bloggers who have the resources for this.

You can also use this tool for proofreading of blog content. Use the Wordy online tool to submit content for review by outsourced proofreaders. The nice benefit of this tool is that a proofreader will review the content in real-time. You'll receive the proofed content in approximately 20 minutes.

These proofreaders can enhance the readability of your content. You can find information on their pricing by visiting www.wordy.com.

Remember that writing posts for social media should be fun. You need to focus on meshing the fun with the practical—and continually post well-proofed content.

Chapter Seven

Hone Your Writing Style to Engage More Twitter Followers

If you want to draw more people to your blog or website, building a strong following on Twitter is a great place to start. It's important to have a specific social media engagement strategy in place. Check out the following ways to hone your writing style so you can engage more twitter followers.

Excel on Twitter with Technology

Google and the National Science Foundation did research to ascertain how various keywords, rhetoric, and sentence structure worked regarding popularity with Twitter users.

You can use this online tool found at **https://chenhaot.com/retweetedmore** to identify which one of two tweets you create would be retweeted more times.

Basically, you write two tweets on a similar topic. Use that tool with its integrated algorithm to identify which tweet will be more well received by your followers.

Ways to Hone Your Writing Style

Writing exciting tweets get more engagement from your followers. You need to give people a reason to follow you. Write with your own unique style, but make sure to implement some of the following ways to hone your writing style to improve follower engagement.

1. Take a Breath and Be Yourself

We all want to promote our brands as bloggers. Just make sure that you aren't trying to be someone other than yourself. People will see through a façade. Don't be afraid to showcase your unique side. Ask questions in your tweets. Share about daily accomplishments. Show your followers who you really are without all the fluff. Be true to yourself.

2. Be Open to Using Humor or Sarcasm

As mentioned earlier in the book, using sarcasm is great. Just steer clear of crossing the line and becoming too offensive. Now, you can share whatever you want to share. However, speaking from experience, if you want to build a brand as a professional blogger—always opt for more class than excessive sarcasm.

Too much sarcasm can be misunderstood. When you find that balance of humor or sarcasm and providing relevant content, that can become a goldmine of new followers and potential new traffic to your blog. **We need to have a focus of always driving traffic to our blogs and getting new subscribers**.

3. Add Some Emotion to Your Tweets

Now, you don't want to get overly emotional and share every deep secret, feeling, and thought. However, bloggers who can convey some emotion in their tweets will start to connect with their followers.

4. Take a Chance and Go Forth Boldly

One of your goals as a blogger on Twitter is to stand out and live on the edge a little. Again, always write with a balance. Don't go too crazy. Someone might misinterpret your tweet and report you for being out of your mind—saying that you need help. Ok, maybe that's an extreme example, but you get the idea. Add just the right amount of boldness to catch your follower's attention and keep them following you.

5. Get Creative When Writing a Call-to-Action

Remember 80 percent of your tweets need to be engaging with followers. For the 20 percent of tweets that promote your blog, get creative with your call-to-action (CTA). You want to compel your followers to check out your blog or website, subscribe to your magazine, or get involved in your cause.

It may seem like a far-off dream to become a superstar on Twitter. Don't give up. My Twitter following grew from 2,500 to 10,200 in just six months. It continues to grow daily. You can start to grow your following by doing the same thing.

Now, I have a number in mind. My number is 50,000. Once I get to 50,000 followers, I won't be following back as many people. I am following approximately 7,800 people now. It can get overwhelming reading my Twitter feed with so many tweets coming all the time. That's why I have a number in mind. You should think of a number that would work well with you.

It is true, that you can gain more followers by following people who follow you. Unless you're a famous writer, actor, singer, or other celebrity, you won't get 1 million followers without starting to follow people back.

I use UnfollowSpy www.unfollowspy.com to manage my Twitter follow and unfollow list. You can only follow or unfollow 100 people per day with this online tool, but it is free—so it's worth it. This tool can help you keep a good balance between who you're following and who's following you. When people don't follow you back, you can log on and easily see who they are and unfollow them. You can add people to a "whitelist" for accounts like news outlets, magazines, or celebrities you want to continue following—even when they don't follow you back. I manually go through the list once a week. However, you can set it up for automatic following and unfollowing.

Chapter Eight

Use Three Simple Formulas to Enhance Your Social Media Content

There are 3.26 billion individuals that use social media each day on their mobile devices. That is a huge untapped resource of potential readers for your blog. Of course, you need to hone your content to your specific target audience.

Having an action plan in place can help you increase your reach on social media. Review the following three basic formulas to see which one or ones you'd like to integrate into your social media content writing strategy.

1. Solve Problems with Your Social Media Content

Improve your engagement on social media by writing posts that solve problems for your followers. Describe a problem your followers may have and detail a simple solution for it.

Get in touch with the "pain points" of your followers.

- For example, as a blogger, you have something that your followers need. You have knowledge of your field of expertise. Get in touch with various groups of followers such as fellow writers, bloggers, or readers. Offer blogging or writing advice. Offer a giveaway such as an ebook or gift card.

2. Stimulate Curiosity in Discovery in Your Followers

People are overwhelmed by information these days. We get emails, texts, notifications from social media posts, and live with a 24-hour news cycle. The readers you are trying to find are also overwhelmed with the same information each day. It is easy for your social media posts to get lost amidst the constantly changing information they digest daily. You need to make a consistent, daily effort to ensure that your content stands out from the crowd.

Stimulate curiosity in your followers to want to discover more about you and your blog. Provide just the right amount of information to whet the appetite of your followers. Just don't give everything away at once. You want to draw them in to your blog. **Getting blog subscribers is your main goal. Don't forget that**.

- For example, share a snippet of how your website ranking has been organically rising in rank. Share how you have been learning some great tips about how to grow your blog readership. Sharing this type of information can spark an interest in discovery. People will start to become interested in what you are offering, and they'll click your "read more" link.

3. Cultivate Reader Engagement by Asking Questions

It seems simple but asking a question on social media platforms like Twitter can spark a discussion. Now, be prepared. Not every question will get a response. However, I have had success with this step. Some questions have gotten a lot of responses. For example, maybe you wrote a Top Ten List about some famous quotes from authors. Promote that blog post with a question like in the following tweet.

- #WritingCommunity Does anyone have any favorite quotes from famous authors to share? My favorite quote is from C.S. Lewis: "You can't get a cup of tea big enough or a book long enough to suit me." Read more quotes from famous authors here. (Then provide the link to your article.)

Solve problems for your readers. Stimulate their curiosity so that they want to get to know you more. Engage with them by asking questions.

Chapter Nine

Use These 3 Social Media Copywriting Tips to Generate More Leads

In 2019, there are 326 million active monthly users on Twitter. Approximately 2.27 billion users are active on Facebook. Instagram has 400 million active users. Have you been generating successful leads with all of these active users on the various social media platforms?

It's important to have the right copywriting strategy in place so you can generate leads on social media. Review the following three social media copywriting tips which can help you get more leads for your blog, books, or whatever you are promoting through your website.

Promote Contests on Social Media

Most people love to get free things. Companies often offer free products to people who are willing to subscribe to their email lists or podcasts, or other reasons. Whenever you are hosting a contest or giveaway, make sure you promote it well on all of your social media accounts. This is a great way to engage with your current followers and gain new followers or leads.

It's important to clearly define the rules of the contest in the post on social media. Of course, you cannot post lengthy content on a platform like Twitter, so make sure you plan out your marketing content accordingly. Convoluted tweets will not get engagement from others.

People are inundated with posts online each day. This is especially true on twitter where tweets on your timeline pop up within seconds—especially if you follow many accounts that post often.

Consider the following example of a post for Facebook sharing information about a restaurant that is hosting a contest. You can use this text as a template and reword it to apply specifically to your book giveaway or whatever other contest you're hosting for your blog.

- We're excited to announce that our new menu is out! All appetizers are offered at ½ price from 4-6 and 9-closing time! You can help us celebrate our new menu by entering our #giveaway. We are giving away 3 $50 GIFT CARDS to our restaurant to three lucky winners. Follow these simple steps to enter to win: Like this post, tag a friend, and share the post. Winners will be announced on Facebook and on our blog on (PROVIDE DATE).

Offer Links to Free Resources

Free things draw in leads. Offer links to free resources such as a white paper, ebook, or list of blog directories. This giveaway should be promoted online on all your social media accounts, and this will bring them to your blog when they click the links. You can use a pop-up window for them to enter their email address and then they'll gain access to the resource—either by being redirected to a link on your site or it will be emailed to them.

This is such an easy way to get new leads just because you gave away a free resource. However, remember that it needs to be worth it. Don't give away something of no value. Otherwise, the leads won't value it and likely will never move further down your sales funnel.

Package the promotional content for the giveaway in the right manner so you quickly attract the right people to click on your link. Consider the following promotional example:

- July 15th is National Give Something Away Day. Take advantage of this day (or others like it on the list in the link at www.nationaltoday.com) to generate new leads online. If you've created an eBook on how to write blog posts that rank higher in SERP, you can promote this tweet on July 15th in honor of this day. Share with your followers that you want to participate by giving something away.

Of course, you can find more quirky "National Days" to celebrate. Some holidays you may want to consider are National Chocolate Chip Day on May 15th or National Pizza Party Day on May 17th.

Create Engaging Live Videos

If you've been on social media for any length of time, you know that many people like to interact and comment on social media posts. You can easily engage your social media following and generate more leads by cultivating your brand as a blogger or writer who engages with followers through videos.

According to statistics, approximately 52 percent of marketers have found that they could significantly increase brand awareness when they used live videos on social media platforms. Consider the following ideas for your video promotion:

- Monday Motivational Content
- Thursday Thoughts or Tips
- Sensational Saturday Stories

Remember that you want to create live video content which engages people and excites them to return to your blog each week to see what helpful or fun information you'll share.

Follow these three simple social media copywriting tips and you can increase lead generation at your blog. Promote contests, share free resources, and post live videos to generate new leads.

Chapter Ten

Mastering the Art Form of Writing Compelling Social Media Posts

If you want to engage a larger audience and connect with more leads for your blog, using social media the right way can be extremely effective. There are currently 2.27 billion active users on Facebook as of January 2021 and 400 million active users per month on Instagram.

When you master the art of writing for the medium of social media, you can increase your reach and engage new readers. Consider the following tips on writing content which can get you the attention that you want to lead people back to your blog.

How to Write Content Geared for the Top Social Media Networks

You need to understand the top social media networks if you want to write compelling content that will convert leads. Google+ closed in April 2019, so you don't need to learn how to write for that platform.

- Facebook
- Instagram
- Twitter
- Pinterest
- LinkedIn

The most popular social network is **Facebook**. This platform sends more traffic to blogs and websites than any of the other five platforms. You can get the best results on Facebook by gearing your content toward entertainment and news.

Write posts with shorter text and interesting images or short videos when writing content for **Instagram**. You likely won't get a lot of traffic to your blog from this platform. However, you should focus on using this platform to enhance your brand as a professional blogger, writer, or author.

If you want to write content that will drive a lot of traffic to your blog—which is why you're reading this blogger mentoring guide—then you should focus attention on cultivating your **Twitter** following. Quickly grab your reader's attention by posting news-worthy content featuring your brand. This will increase the chances of getting your content retweeted and responded to—and improve your click-through-rate (CTR).

If sharing fun and engaging photos interests you, then focus on using **Pinterest** to post photos and pictures that people will pin to their boards. Many people pin photos for inspiration. Think about content that will inspire people and include memorable tag lines.

When you post content on **LinkedIn**, you need to remember that this is a social media platform geared for professionals. The dynamic is much different than all the other platforms. You can use this platform to share interesting blog posts or articles you've written. Write catchy headlines and a brief promo blurb about the article or post to increase the chance of catching people's interest as they scroll through their newsfeed.

Get Creative with Post Content for Social Media Platforms

It's been mentioned already in this guide that you should engage with followers 80 percent of the time and only promote 20 percent. However, it's an important point to make so it bears repeating.

People don't want you to sell to them. They want to get to know you and your brand. They want to have a reason to go to your blog. You need to give them that reason and be your own unique and engaging self.

Consider some of the following ways that you can get creative with your social media content.

- When sharing your blog post link, include an **engaging question** or interesting text that encourages people to click your link.
- Show your **unique personality** and enhance your brand image by posting visually engaging behind-the-scenes photos of yourself.
- When you post **interesting, curated content** from others in your field, remember to credit them as a source. This is another way to connect with your followers because you are providing them with interesting and educational information.

- **News sells**—especially in our current culture with its 24-hour news cycle online. Share relevant news articles and comment when you retweet.

Writing compelling social media posts is an important step in cultivating your brand online and drawing traffic to your blog and website.

Chapter Eleven

Use These Simple Copywriting Tips to Increase Conversion Rates

The average website has a 2.35 percent conversion rate for leads clicking through the call-to-action (CTA) links. The conversion rate is 3-5 times higher for websites that rank in the top 10 percent of online searches.

You can begin implementing these tips to start increasing the conversion rate for your online content on your blog or website.

1. Write Strong Headlines that Quickly Grab the Reader's Attention

Writing superior content is the basic building block of increasing your conversion rates. You may think this sounds like a simple solution to get more leads to sign up for your newsletter or buy your books. However, writing copy that converts is not as easy as it sounds. You can't settle for mediocre content and hope that it converts just because you stuff it with keywords and use other optimization techniques.

Well-known content creator, Neil Patel suggests that high-quality, original content will rank higher with the new Google's algorithm updates. Such relevant helpful content is likely to appeal more to visitors and then increase conversion rates.

Headlines are so important since approximately 80 percent of people read them. Only 20 percent of readers click through to read the content. Make sure every word you write counts so people will read your blog content.

2. Be Careful with Placement of Images and CTA in Your Content

Combine the right words, dynamic images, and the CTA in the perfect placement in your content to get the best conversion results. Craft the perfect pathway to guide the reader to want to respond to your CTA and be sent to the purchase point.

You need to find the right balance of content and visuals. It's important that you don't distract the reader with too many images. With the perfect mix of content and photos, you can easily help your readers hone in on the CTA. If they get too distracted from that pathway, you won't increase your conversion rate.

3. Stay Focused on Delivering a Clear and Concise Message

Joanne Wiebe coined the term conversion copywriter because she wanted to identify the best techniques for increasing your conversion by writing better copy. If you stay on track with your messaging, that's another significant way to increase your conversion rate. You want to deliver a clear and concise message so the reader can quickly identify your CTA and follow through.

Be persuasive without making your reader feel like you're forcing them to comply with your CTA. You want to persuade them so that *they* decide to continue reading and responding to your call-to-action. When readers feel like they are in control, they are more likely to comply with what you're asking them to do.

You must be totally focused on persuading your readers to complete an action if you want your conversion copywriting to work correctly. You may want readers to take some of the following actions:

- Subscribe to your email newsletter
- Click an internal link on your website
- Share your content on social media
- Make a product or service purchase

Always write high-quality content to maximize your powers of persuasion. You can easily apply conversion copywriting to any articles, blog posts, emails, or website content you write.

Remember to always write strong headlines and stay steadfast and strategic in image and CTA placement. Don't stray from your message or your readers will get distracted. You want your readers to be just as focused on your message as you are.

Chapter Twelve

Conquer Your Content Niche with These 8 Tips

You can effectively reach today's consumer by writing niche content that is geared toward specific topics. With so many online searches today, writing niche content is a great way to get more traffic to your blog or website. Review the following eight strategies that can help you effectively conquer your content niche and reach more readers.

1. Originality is a Key Component

The first step is to start with original content that educates the reader and provides value. Now, this true for all content. However, it is especially true when writing for your specific niche market. Maybe your blog is about book reviews, but more specifically you only review Christian novels in the romantic suspense genre. That means that all your content is geared toward reviews in this genre, and you need to create interesting and unique reviews with relevant keywords.

The search ranking algorithm, Panda, was implemented online by Google in 2011. As of 2019 and with their recent updates to this algorithm, higher quality content is even more valuable in ranking higher in SERP. It's important to note that low-quality content is prevented from ranking higher in SERP by the algorithm.

Make sure every blog post counts. Don't just post a blog every day because you want to get content online. If it's not high-quality content, you could significantly decrease your ranking—especially if this is a habit. Remember the following factors which the algorithm looks for when identifying high-quality content online:

- Content word length
- Proper spelling and grammar
- Keyword density that avoids stuffing
- Use of niche specific keywords

As you start to write more quality content, you should begin to see an increase in your SERP ranking. I have seen significant ranking increases by following these steps. The information I'm providing here works—when properly applied to your specific blog or website.

2. Get Inside the Head of Your Readers

Generally, people write content online to get readers to follow a Call-to-Action (CTA). Maybe you are writing a blog post because you want to generate more traffic to your blog or maintain the current readership base. Some people write online content to improve their brand image or to sell products.

However, you cannot truly reach readers if you are selling to them in your content. You need to provide educational value with every blog post you publish on your site. Educate them. Connect with readers. Cultivate a relationship that is built on trust. This will help you to increase your conversion rate.

Make a concerted effort during the writing and editing process to ensure that you are focused on delivering superior quality niche content that readers are looking for. This can help you stand out from your competition and improve your brand image as a professional blogger.

If you don't understand your audience, you cannot effectively write content that resonates with them. Consider following this strategy to get to know your target audience better:

- Complete marketing research
- Review analytics pre and post publication
- Target an emotional connection with the reader

Don't get discouraged. Mastering this process of balancing creativity with market research will take time. However, as you practice this balancing act, the process will get easier, and you will gain more traffic and convert more leads.

3. Fully Embrace a Deeper Subset of Your Niche

Some top content niche markets include the following: relationships, pets, finances, weight loss, prepping, and babies. You can conquer your content niche by fully embracing a deeper subset of it. For example, maybe you have a blog where you write content about babies. Consider focusing on a subset of the niche like parenting for millennials or advice for adoptive and foster parents. When you celebrate your audience, you can find a way to speak their language and provide content that answers their specific information needs.

4. Write Stellar Content That is Worthy of Back Links

If you want to create high-quality content, you must include invaluable information like infographics, statistics, and quotes from experts. We've already introduced Neil Patel earlier. He is a high-ranking marketer and blogger who wrote an article about SEO. In this article, he linked back to several other sites which included quality, comprehensive data and studies. This information helped him prove various points in his article.

Ten years ago, backlinks were more valuable for SEO than they are today. However, they still hold value today since the Google search algorithm identifies backlinks and sees that people are linking to your site. That means people find value in your information. This increases your SERP ranking. Anytime you use backlinks in your articles, make sure your use related keywords.

5. Learn Your Craft and Write Consistent Niche Content

Neil Patel reports that writing high-quality content on a consistent basis can improve your lead generation by up to 126 percent. The odds are in your favor if you start consistently publishing great content. Remember the following points when writing niche content:

- Rank higher online with longer articles or blog posts
- Cultivate trust with readers by providing consistent niche content
- Improve your image as a professional blogger with constant content

6. Don't Be Afraid to Use Jargon Specific to Your Niche

When you write niche content, you should know jargon specific to your area of expertise—especially if you want your content to resonate with your target audience. Using such jargon will help you when optimizing the content to compete better in SERP. Readers and the Google algorithm will start to see you and your content as an expert in the field. This will serve to improve your online ranking.

Consider what jargon a blogger writing for the marketing field would need to know and include in their content:

- KPI – Key Performance Indicator
- Keywords
- Gated Content
- CTA – Call-to-Action

7. Always Focus on Educating the Reader

Educate the reader by providing invaluable content that they cannot find anywhere else. Of course, you will have competition and similar content will be found online. However, you need to find a way to educate your readers by showcasing your unique voice as an expert in your field.

Don't puff yourself up or say you're an expert if you're not. Remember to always be true with your credentials. No one is saying that you must have a Ph.D., but you need to back up your content with the right statistics or expert quotes. You will need to become a diligent researcher.

Immerse yourself in the following resources to fully educate yourself:

- Videos posted on YouTube from experts in your field
- Data and information from reputable websites in your field
- Review authoritative blog sites and magazines

For example, if you are writing a blog post on a marketing topic, you should research the top marketing blogs so you can familiarize yourself with the field. Review this listing of the top marketing blogs which were chosen by marketers.

8. Believe What You're Writing So Readers Believe You

If you don't believe in what you're writing, readers will easily pick up on that. Get well-informed on your niche market so you can become more confident as you write. The more you research, the more easily the words will spill out onto the screen—and you'll soon start feeling like an expert yourself.

Sharing facts will help your readers gain a deeper sense of confidence in your work. They will trust you. When a reader trusts your content, they will subscribe to your site and become repeat visitors. Soon, they will convert to follow your CTAs.

You will meet Google's quality guidelines when you write trustworthy content that adds value to the reader and meets search requests online.

Following this strategy can significantly increase the chances that your content will start to rank higher in search engine results.

Chapter Thirteen

13 Effective SEO Techniques You Should Implement

Rule the internet and increase your ranking on Search Engine Results Pages (SERP) by creating optimized and relevant content. Check out this list of important SEO techniques that you should start implementing today.

1. Learn All You Can About Your Audience and What They Want

You've probably heard SEO and marketing experts say how important it is to know your target audience. They are not wrong. It is extremely vital to learn all about your audience and understand what they want.

When you know what your audience wants and what they need, it makes it easier to provide them with the relevant content and cultivate a long-lasting blogger and reader relationship. Identifying whether your readers prefer video content, images, or longer text can be an invaluable resource for you in reaching your audience. You can provide quality, optimized content, but if it's not what your readers are looking for—then your CTR and conversion rates will not significantly increase.

2. Focus on Providing High-Quality Content

As mentioned many times in this guide book, updates to the Google algorithm showed that high-quality content would improve SERP ranking. Steer clear of posting mediocre blog posts each day. Write superior content that will grab the attention of both readers and the Google algorithm.

Once you identify the best way to connect with your audience and continually deliver superior, relevant content that meets their needs—you'll rank higher in SERP. Make sure you use images, subheadings, bullet points, and numbered lists to enhance the readability factor and shareability of posts.

It sounds like I'm constantly hammering home the fact that you need to provide high-quality content in order to rank higher in SERP, but that's a fact. You can review Google's Search Quality Evaluation Guidelines which Google Search Quality Evaluators use when they rate online content. However, you probably don't have time to read through that 164-page document. So, keep reading this article for tips on how to optimize content on your blog or website. The journey begins with high-quality content.

All blog or website content must be clearly defined to help increase your online ranking. For the purposes of URL ranking, the algorithm focuses mostly on landing page content. Additionally, the reputation of the brand or site creator is also considered by the algorithm regarding page quality rating.

Keep in mind the importance of the following three factors when creating content:

- Expertise
- Authority
- Trustworthiness

As the content creator for your blog or website, make sure you exhibit expertise and authority in your field. If you publish Your Money or Your Life (YMYL) content on your site, the algorithm deems it as more trustworthy if the information is written by a financial expert or nutritionist.

3. Create Reader Friendly Content

Write content targeted to your readership base that answers the intent of their online keyword searches. This can provide a great user experience (UX). Make sure all the content on your website or blog is easy to navigate. If it is not user-friendly and doesn't provide relevant internal links to keep users on the site, they'll leave. This increases your bounce rate—which decreases your SERP ranking. Make content more readable by using the following:

- Header and subheaders
- Bullet points and numbered lists
- Images, Infographics, and Videos
- Shorter two-four sentence paragraphs

4. Optimize Site with Higher Speeds

Website load speed is an important factor for providing a superior user experience and for the Google algorithm when ranking for SERP. Less sites can be crawled by search engines when they load too slowly. So, faster speeds are rewarded. According to Google web developers, they suggest web designers use CSSNano and UglifyJS when optimizing website code.

5. Focus on Search Engine Structure

Google, Yandex, Microsoft, and Yahoo created Schema.org in 2011. This structure was designed to provide a uniform listing of entities and qualities which all their search engines would support. Focus on catering to search engine structure as you optimize online content for 2019 and into next year. Artificial intelligence (AI) has become even more integral to the operation of the Google algorithm. Be intentional when crafting metadata and tags which are added to the HTML markup on your site—and help search engines better "understand" your content.

Adding structured data to the HTML markup on your page is an important step in SEO. Search engines use these short pieces of information from the structured data to generate content when your site is shown in SERP.

6. Ensure that Your Website is Mobile-Friendly

Google shared on their blog about mobile-first indexing at the end of 2016. Prior to that time, their algorithm had focused on analyzing desktop versions of websites. Since so many people check websites on their mobile phones and tablets, Google shifted their focus to mobile-first indexing. In the future, Google will only use a site's mobile version for ranking. So, you should get started now with ensuring that your website is mobile-friendly.

Carefully review your website platform to find out if they are a dynamic serving / responsive site. These types of platforms enable a great UX through mobile-friendly viewing. Basically, it's best if you use a website platform that enables easy navigation for you to edit content on both the desktop and mobile viewing—and offers easy navigation for viewers on mobile devices like phones and tablets.

With Google's Structured Data Testing Tool, you can use it to easily detect errors in the output across platforms. This tool provides relevant debugging and monitoring reports. You can test the rendering and availability of the structured data indexing.

7. Get Content Ready for Voice Search

According to research completed by OC&C Strategy Consultants, they estimate that there will be a $40 billion jump in consumers using voice shopping by 2022. Approximately 50 percent of all searches will be completed through voice search by 2020. You will lose site traffic if your website or blog has not been optimized for voice searching. Sites not optimized for voice search will not achieve the Needs Met (NM) rating by the Google algorithm.

When users search online with a typed query, they typically input more words than if they did a voice search. Additionally, when people speak, it is generally more conversational in tone than when they type in a search. Make sure your content is now optimized for more informal voice searches.

8. Ensure Optimized Content for a Better UX

Again, it's so important to provide a superior user experience (UX) when optimizing content. Providing boring content is a surefire way to bore readers and increase the bounce rates. That negatively impacts page quality rating. Optimize the site for the following:

- Provide a quick and enjoyable conversion process for leads
- Ensure user-friendly internal site search capabilities with relevant content
- Implement chatbots to enhance the user experience and improve procedures
- Utilize user-friendly email forms and purchasing processes
- Add descriptive text for alt text so search engines can identify photos

Include on-page optimization in your strategy for higher ranking in search engine results pages (SERP). Provide content that effectively answers basic user questions. It is important that users get relevant content on your blog or website when they put in specific keywords online. All conversion processes on your site such as subscribing to a newsletter, sharing a post, completing a form, or buying a product must be simple and easy to navigate. Ensure a smooth process with chatbots.

9. Embrace the Trend of Machine Learning

According to SEO Tribunal, each day, 15 percent of search engine queries processed by Google are new. The Google RankBrain algorithm uses machine learning to identify the best match to queries. This machine learning technology was only used in that small percentage of queries that the algorithm had never "heard" before.

However, Google has been rebranding themselves as a "Machine Learning First" company. Machine learning is a trend of the SEO future.

Currently, the foundation is being laid for search engines to utilize machine learning to respond to user *intents* instead of their *actual* questions. You need to stay informed about the future impact that machine learning will have on search results.

10. Optimize Content for The Best Google Search Experience

Focus on creating content and optimizing it to provide the best user experience for people searching on Google. Be intentional when creating meta descriptions and page titles which will be displayed more visually in Search Engine Results Pages (SERP) listings.

Enhance the title content and snippets to be shown to increase your click-through rate (CTR). Optimize your content with this SERP Snippet Optimization Tool. You need to have a SERP listing for your site that is more appealing than your competitors—so people click through.

People search online and type a question in the browser on Google. The SERP will generally feature ten sites on each page. A variety of content will show on the SERP such as Google SERP features, paid advertisements, and organic listings. Tailor your optimization efforts for SERP features such as the following:

- featured snippets
- direct answer boxes
- bulleted lists
- numbered lists
- tables and videos

The Google algorithm pulls information from your website and reformats the content for listings in SERPs. You can pre-format your content for SERP features. For example, a blog post that includes a subheading and a target keyword—with a bullet list near the top of the content (above the fold)—can be easily pulled by the Google algorithm to be included in an SERP Bullet Featured Snippet.

11. Improve Site Ranking by Using Brand Identity

According to web trend analyst Gary Illyes, you can improve your brand by having your content shared by others on social networks. This improved branding can also increase your online ranking. Artificial intelligence (AI) is used by the Google algorithm to analyze and learn good versus bad content that has been disseminated online. You can make connections with brand influencers, pay attention to what your competitors are doing, and make a diligent effort to enhance your brand identity a blogger.

12. Use Technology to Bring Your Website to the Next Level

The features and designs of website platforms have become more complex in recent years. When you implement a technical SEO strategy, you can take your website to the next level. Sites that have a higher load speed are rewarded with a higher ranking by the Google algorithm. Google is the major search engine that most online searchers use. This search engine works best with web platforms that are driven by the web programming language, JavaScript which updates and changes CSS and HTML.

13. Take a Multifaceted SEO Approach

This last point may not pertain to you as a blogger. However, if you ever decide to develop your own app or have one developed for you, then you should remember the information shared here.

Companies or brands that have apps available in the Apple Store, Google Play Store, and Amazon App Store need to find ways to optimize their app for increased visibility. Many more people use mobile devices to search online. Make sure it's easy for users to easily search for your apps in app stores. As previously mentioned, it is important to ensure that your website and blog is mobile friendly.

Take the time to review this comprehensive listing of 13 important SEO techniques to identify which ones you can begin implementing. As you start applying each of these steps, you should begin to see your website or blog ranking increase.

Chapter Fourteen

Tips on How to Increase the Speed of Your WordPress Site

We've already established that if you want your site to increase in online ranking, you need to create high-quality content that is relevant to reader's keyword searches.

However, slow loading websites can significantly decrease traffic to the site. People want to browse websites that have a fast page load time. According to a 2017 Google Page Load Time Study, your bounce rate will significantly decrease by up to 123 percent if your site loads in under three seconds.

You want your bounce rate to be low, not high. If it's high, that means people are quickly "bouncing" from your website—because it was not interesting, they couldn't find the right information they were looking for, or the site was not easy to navigate.

An excellent bounce rate is 26-40 percent. The average bounce rate is 41-55 percent. A worse than average bounce rate is 56-70 percent. This may not necessarily be alarming, depending on the website. A disappointing bounce rate is 70 percent and higher.

The Recommended Load Time for Websites and Blogs

Since you need a fast site load time to increase in ranking with Google's search algorithm, it's important to note that the recommended load time is 1.9 seconds or less. If you want to increase your online ranking, all images, HTML, CSS, and JavaScript must load within the initial rendering period of less than 1.9 seconds.

Increase WordPress Site Page Load Time

Now, I don't use WordPress for my website and blog. I use Wix, which I really like and haven't had any major issues with. However, many people use WordPress, so I wanted to share some of the following ways to increase WordPress site speed by optimizing images, using optimized themes, and faster WordPress plug-ins.

1. Focus on the Theme – Use optimized themes to create a faster WordPress site to increase page load time. Here are some of the following optimized WordPress themes which you can use: MagPlus, Divi, Gillion, Soledad, and Jevelin.

2. Optimized Plug-ins – Faster website speeds will help you gain more subscribers, increase traffic, and ensure that visitors are happier. Use optimized WordPress plugins to improve page speed. Consider using some of the following speed enhancing plugins: WP Super Minify, BJ Lazy Load, Perfmatters, WP Rocket, Cache Enabler, and WP Super Cache.

3. Use Optimized Images – It is important to optimize images to increase the website load speed. We need to continually be cognizant of increasing our site page speed score. You should choose the right image format to save space and resize the image prior to uploading.

4. PageSpeed Tools by Google – Google PageSpeed Tools can provide invaluable information when you need to analyze the current webpage speed on all devices such as laptops, PCs, tablets, and cell phones. Enter the website URL so the tool can analyze the speed. Google developers created tools such as PageSpeed Insights and Modules for speeding up PageSpeed.

Chapter Fifteen

A Guide to Optimizing a WordPress Blog for Google

As I mentioned in the previous chapter, I work with the Wix platform. This chapter delves into more details on how to optimize a WordPress blog for Google. Now, some of the information shared here is exclusive for WordPress blogs and some can be applied to other blog platforms as well.

Setting up your WordPress blog is simple if you've followed the navigation setup and operation process. However, there is more to simply setting up your blog. You need to optimize your site for higher ranking in Google Search Engine Result Pages (SERP).

Yes, there is quite a lot of repetition in this guide regarding various SEO strategies. However, I feel that is good since it will hammer home the importance of effectively optimizing your blog or website if you want it to increase in online ranking.

Consider the following basic SEO strategies to implement:

- Create high-quality content
- Write in a conversational tone
- Use subheadings and images
- Include bullet points and lists
- Link to related sites
- Use keywords and meta tags

Starting with those basic SEO steps is a great way to begin to see increased online ranking and an increase in organic traffic. However, there is more that you can do with your WordPress blog to rank higher in SERP. Consider implementing the following advanced strategies to boost ranking.

1. Focus on Speeding Up Your Site

In the previous chapter, we discussed that your site should load in 3 seconds or less. Sites that load within 1-2 seconds rank even higher in SERP. As mentioned, load time includes how fast all elements on your website like CSS, JavaScript, HTML, and images load.

Consider the following easy steps to improve page loading speed on WordPress:

- Utilize optimized themes with fast load times
- Optimize images to load faster
- Use faster plugins like Sucuri Firewall, W3 Total Cache, WP Rocket, and WP Super Cache

People want to browse sites that load quickly. Approximately, 53 percent of people will leave a website if it takes longer than three seconds to fully load.

2. Use an XML Sitemap on Your Blog

NOTE: This tip can be used for all blogs, not just WordPress sites. Make it easier for Google to find all the pages on your blog or website by using an XML sitemap. These sitemap tags will improve crawl times for the Google algorithm to find your content.

Sitemaps for media content like images and videos can be used as well to ensure indexing of this media. When you use sitemaps, they can aid in monitoring search engine performance. You can review whether or not your pages have been indexed by Google. WordPress users can use the Google XML Sitemaps plugin on their blog.

For platforms other than WordPress, you can select your site on the Google Console home page. Move to the menu on the left and click "sitemaps." In the text field next to your domain, type in "sitemap.xml" and then click submit.

3. Don't Forget About Optimizing Your Old Posts

You should link to old posts on your blog when you write new content. Integrating internal links into new content provides more relevant information on your site for the search engines to crawl.

Additionally, providing internal links on new content gives site readers more reasons to stay on your website or blog. That improves your bounce rate and helps to increase your online ranking. If you use plugins for your WordPress blog to link to older posts, that will show the complete title. It's better to manually enter these links with relevant anchor text so you can have a seamless transition from the new text to the link to the old text. You can boost traffic to new posts as well as older posts with internal linking.

4. Optimize the Site for Mobile Viewing

Make sure you have added the tracking code from Google Analytics to accurately track visitors to your blog and website. You can find out important percentages such as the percent of people viewing your site on desktop, mobile, and tablet

Many people are accessing websites and blogs through their phones and tablets. Make sure your blog is optimized with a Responsive Web Design (RWD). With such a design, the site will render well on all devices.

You'll provide a superior user experience (UX) since readers of your blog and website will be able to view and access all content on all devices—even mobile phones. Many times, the desktop version will show up well on a tablet. However, if you are not using an RWD, it will not be mobile-friendly on a cell phone.

If your site has an RWD, it will qualify for increased ranking with the updated Google algorithm. One of the factors the algorithm considers is UX, so make sure the site is mobile-friendly.

For people using the WordPress platform, any of the following default themes with responsive designs is mobile-friendly:

- Twenty Eleven
- Twenty Twelve
- Twenty Thirteen

5. Fix Broken Links on the Site

Broken links or dead links lead to unavailable pages. These may be broken internal links or external links in articles you've written. Maybe you typed the link incorrectly or the link is now unavailable and shows a 4xx or 5xx status code.

It is detrimental to your online ranking if the Google algorithm identifies too many broken links on your site. Your website may be penalized by search engines because it is deemed inadequately maintained.

You can use the Broken Link Checker WordPress plugin to manage any issues with external or internal broken links on your blog. The plugin can be set to automatically list these broken links as "nofollow." Then the search engine algorithms won't think your site is unmaintained. You will be notified by email if the plugin detects any broken links on your site. You can then easily navigate through the plugin interface to correct the URLs or unlink to them.

You can also use this website **https://www.brokenlinkcheck.com** to check for broken links on your site. It will review all indexed pages and let you know which ones have broken links. Then, you can go to those pages and either fix an incorrect link or delete a broken link.

Review your WordPress blog and implement these optimization strategies. Then make sure you track web traffic statistics to find out if site traffic has increased. Use an online tool like WebRankStats, Alexa Rank, or SEMRush to track if your blog continues to increase in rank and if these SEO strategies are working for you

Chapter Sixteen

Diving Deeper into Site Optimization

You have a blog, but you need visitors. You won't make any money from ads or anything you're selling—like blogger mentoring or site subscriptions through a venue like SubscribeStar—if you don't have consistent and repeat web traffic. Let's face facts. Your blog is in competition with the over 1.94 billion websites online for the approximately 4.1 billion global internet users. Going by these numbers, the odds are not in your favor.

We've discussed integrating such search engine optimization (SEO) techniques like fixing broken links, keyword research, boosting page speed, enhancing the overall user experience (UX), augmenting content for voice searches, and creating a mobile-ready site.

Let's consider some other important ways to develop the search engine results pages (SERP) for your site.

1. Identify the Rank of Your Website

Identifying the current ranking of your website and blog is an important initial step in developing your SERP space. Run an analysis on your site with Alexa so you can ascertain your ranking, as well as the strengths and weakness of the site—and other statistics like referral sources and engagement metrics.

2. Learn the Basic Search Types

People make three basic types of searches online. The first search is **informational** where people search for content on different topics. The second type of search is called **navigational**. With this search, people want to find a specific brand, but they are not sure of the specific URL. The third search is called **transactional** which is related to e-commerce sites. The person searching wants to purchase a product or service online.

You should review SERPs for your competition by doing whichever type of search applies to you. As a blogger, **your key focus would be on informational searches**.

When you see what other bloggers are doing and what keywords they are ranking for, that can help you know what keywords you should focus on—and don't forget to include long tail keywords to increase your chances of ranking and meeting people's informational needs.

3. Only Publish Quality Content

All content published online is evaluated by Google's Search Quality Evaluators and rated for page quality according to factors listed in their E-A-T guidelines. Demonstrate expertise, authoritativeness, and trustworthiness in your content and it will receive a higher rating.

4. Build on a Solid Foundation

Search engine bots crawl the web to identify authoritative content that answers search results that people are searching for. Make sure you have authoritative foundational pages on your website that deliver more value than an average blog post.

You can write a white paper on a topic in your field of expertise. White papers run between 3,000 – 5,000 words and are very detailed and provide high value for the reader. You can then offer a free ebook download at the end of the white paper so readers can then subscribe to your email newsletter or blog posts.

5. Increase Reader Engagement

If you want to increase traffic to your website, you need to write content that is meeting the needs of internet searches. Obviously, your blog won't meet the billions of searches on Google each day. However, you need to optimize your content and work diligently to get to page 1 on SERPs for your blog.

You can increase reader engagement by writing in a conversational tone in a laidback style. Don't forget about bullet lists, headers, images, infographics, and other ways to create visually appealing content.

6. Create Blog Titles That Convert

Write dynamic titles that will make your SERP space stand out from your competition and increase your click-through-rate (CTR). Remember to use concise and engaging content, rich in keywords.

7. Write Keyword Rich Meta Descriptions

Effectively summarize the content in a meta description. You can use up to 155 characters in a tag in HTML. When someone searches for specific keywords that are in your meta description, your blog post or webpage content shows up in the search. Improve your SERP space by writing a great meta description that includes relevant keywords to impact the reader for better engagement.

8. Seamlessly Integrate Anchor Text

You need to seamlessly integrate the right anchor text when linking to both external and internal content in your articles. Don't just use "click here" for any links. Use relevant keywords that search engine crawlers can process, so your content has more of a chance of increasing rank online.

Chapter Seventeen

Understanding GDPR and How It Will Affect Your Site

The General Data Protection (GDPR) regulation was designed to ensure a simplified and unified approach to how personal data is protected by companies located in Europe—as well as companies or brands that do business with any EU residents.

With the enactment of the updated GDPR EU regulation, you may be wondering what this has to do with your blog or website—especially if you live in the United States.

Review the following information to better understand the relationship between GDPR and online content so you can be ready to handle any impact on your brand as a professional blogger.

Enhanced Lead Engagement

Don't view the new GDPR EU regulation as a stumbling block for marketing your online content and implementing lead generation strategies. Of course, you must make sure you comply with obtaining definitive permission from leads that decide to opt-in to your lead funnels and lists.

Internet privacy expert Simon Carroll said, "When someone grants permission they are acting consciously, becoming an active participant rather than a passive source of data to be pillaged."

A central factor in content marketing for your blog, is to get a lead's permission to interact with them through further engagement. You need to respect the lead and treat them as if they were already a paying subscriber to your blog or educational content. Since more personal data is freely provided rather than you having to gather it online through searches—you can enhance the way you engage with them.

Three Important Factors

It may seem a bit overwhelming to ensure that your online content strategy is compliant with the updated GDPR EU regulation. Focus on three important factors regarding the way data is used. You can positively impact your brand as a professional blogger through improved lead and subscriber engagement.

- **Get Specific Permission** – You must make certain that you have specific opt-ins in place before sending any email content to leads or subscribers. Of course, this GDPR only applies to your interactions with European leads and subscribers. However, it is still a good practice to have opt-ins in place on your lead generation forms and subscribe boxes.

  All lead forms must include an opt-in box for leads to check off clarifying they agree with your privacy policy and terms—so you can be GDPR compliant. Use an opt-in box for promotional materials you send such as email newsletters and other brand information. You cannot simply include a note under the contact information that the lead agrees to your terms and privacy policy when they respond to your free trial. That is not GDPR compliant. They need to check an opt-in box.

- **Make Data Easily Accessible** – One of the ways to comply with GDPR regulations is to ensure that any leads and subscribers have the "right to be forgotten." The updated regulation gives leads and subscribers the chance to maintain control over how their personal data is obtained and used. This means people have easy access to their data if they want to "invoke their right to be forgotten" and have their data removed from your databases.

  According to the "right to be forgotten" ruling from EU Justice Court, you need to give your leads or subscribers easy access to their data. For example, make sure you have a user-friendly unsubscribe link in all emails to leads and subscribers. A second way to comply is to integrate links to user profiles. With this access, subscribers can easily manage email preferences like opting in or out for promotions, special offers, invitations, and important messages.

- **Simplify Data Collection** – You need data from leads, who then become subscribers, in order to thrive in the blogging industry. You will have a harder time of increasing your conversion rates and cultivating positive engagement with leads and subscribers if you don't have an easy way to obtain personal data like contact information and what they like etc.

  By complying with GDPR, you must streamline data collection—so you only collect necessary relevant data. You can't begin collecting all types of personal data you think you need, but which is not proven relevant to current and future engagements with the lead or subscriber. You may think this is overkill. However, if you are not able to provide a relevant reason for obtaining that data, you should not collect it. Focus only on data you specifically need and forget about extraneous details.

Make sure you comply with these regulations. Do not contact leads or subscribers who haven't specifically opted-in to receive your brand content.

Flybe sent emails to over 3.3 million people who had been listed in their database. They wanted to identify whether or not they had the correct details. However, the Information Commissioner's Office fined them since these subscribers had previously unsubscribed from any contact from the company. Once they had unsubscribed, these people should have been removed from the database.

Make sure you keep up with having only active leads and subscribers on lists in your database. Follow the basic rule of only communicating with leads or subscribers who have opted-in for communication with you and you'll easily comply with the updated GDPR. Ensure that all data like their usernames, passwords, and email addresses are easily accessible in your database—and that they can unsubscribe if desired—to ensure compliance.

Chapter 18

Website Link Tools, Important Technical Tips, and a Recap

As a recap, these are the most important ranking tips out of a listing of 200+ Google Ranking Factors.

- Prominent domains backlinking to your site
- Increasing organic click-through-rates
- High authority of Your Domain
- Mobile-friendly viewing
- High number of longer site visits
- Creating high-quality content
- Optimized pages for better Search Engine Crawling

Blog Topic Generator

If you are having trouble brainstorming ideas for blog topics you can use the blog topic generator from HubSpot for help. Simply input some nouns and it will generate several topic ideas. https://www.hubspot.com/blog-readers

Generating JSON-LD Code

JSON-LD code stands for JavaScript Object Notation for Linked Data. This code is a WC3 standard website process for implementing structured data. The code has a simplistic application that is less liable to human errors. A ranked system of name-value pairs is used by this code.

There are several JSON-LD code generators available online for people who are not tech-savvy and don't know how to code. When a code is generated, you add it to the HTML in your header. Some website platforms like Wix will have you add the code in the back office for their advanced SEO settings.

I used the following code generator website to generate a JSON-LD code for my website: https://jsonld.com/json-ld-generator. You can also visit this website https://sitechecker.pro/json-ld-markup to check for any JSON-LD code errors on your site.

Meta Tags with Script

You can provide optimized information to search engines by ensuring that your meta tags with script are added to your website header and in the advanced SEO settings of your site platform.

Check with this support page from Google on how to create meta tags that Google understands: https://support.google.com/webmasters/answer/79812?hl=en. It's important to have the following information in the meta tags:

- Title Tag
- Description Tag
- Keywords Tag

This is an example of what a meta tag would look like for your blog. All sites have their own specific information added to the code (see words in bold). However, the basic code such as "meta name" etc. should be listed. You need to go to Google Search Console at this link: https://search.google.com/search-console/about to get your Google site verification code, which is the listed in the meta tags with script below.

<meta name=**"Writer Blog"** content="HTML, CSS, XML, XHTML, JavaScript"/>
<meta name=**"The Writing Life"** content=**"Blog publishing writing tips and writing journey articles"**>
<meta name="author" content=**"Lisa Smith"**/>
<meta name="google-site-verification"
Content=**"googleed09c75ed06b9915.html"**/>
<meta name="Keywords" content=**"writing advice, writing life, writing tips, writing journey, blogging tips, blogging life"**>
<meta name="viewport" content="width=device-width, initial-scale=1.0"/>

Canonical Tag

A canonical tag is also known as "rel canonical" and it's a method for search engines to identify that a certain URL is relevant to specific content found online on that site. This tag is useful in preventing issues that could arise from duplicate content found on various URLs.

<link rel="canonical" href="{https://www.**lisasmith**.com/}"/>

Creating Structured Data

You can use the Google Structured Data Markup Helper tool to help you create the right structured data markup for your blog and website.

Find the tool on the following website: https://www.google.com/webmasters/markup-helper/

Submitting Site Maps to Google

You need to submit a site map to Google so that it makes it easier for your content to be crawled by Google.

Visit Google Search Console (https://search.google.com/search-console/about) to complete the following tasks:

- Need to have your site verified first (see Google Console)
- Go to Google Search Console home page to select your site.
- From the menu on the left, click sitemaps.
- In the text field next to your domain, type in sitemap.xml.
- Click Submit.

You can also use Google Search Console to check site and URL performance and to ascertain how well individual pages perform.

Link Reclamation Process

You can visit the following link to read an article on how to locate mentions of your website or blog. Then you can ask the site for reclamation—for link building purposes. https://builtvisible.com/link-reclamation-how-to-find-mentions-you-can-turn-into-links/

Finding Keywords and Search Patterns

You can use the following tools to help with finding keywords and search trends and patterns for online web users. This real-world trend data can help you write content that is rich in the right keywords that your target audience is searching for. This can help you write optimized content that will rank higher in SERP.

GOOGLE CORRELATE: https://www.google.com/trends/correlate

LSI (LATENT SEMANTIC INDEXING): https://lsikeywords.com

KEYWORD RANK CHECK: https://smallseotools.com/keyword-position

KEYWORD TOOLS: https://keywordtool.io and https://ads.google.com/home/tools/keyword-planner

Bounce Rate

Remember that you want to have a lower bounce rate since that means website users are staying on your site for a longer time. That provides a better UX and a higher SERP.

You can identify your current bounce rate by visiting Google Analytics: https://analytics.google.com/analytics/web on a regular basis. Site stats are updated after midnight for the prior day. However, you must have the Google Analytics tracking code in the HTML in the header on your website for site traffic and data to be tracked.

Check out the percentages of bounce rates from excellent to disappointing:

26-40% = Excellent
41-55% = Average
56-70% = Worse than Average
70%+ = Disappointing

Session Duration

The longer the session, the more it helps to increase your page quality rating and then increases online ranking. The Google algorithm thinks that your readers are getting value from your site because they are staying on the site a long time.

3-15 minutes = Excellent
30 seconds – 2 minutes = Good

Less than 15 seconds = bad

That's why it's good to have longer blog posts—that are reader-friendly with bullet lists, subheadings, images, and infographics—so that site visits are longer.

Create Deeper Content

Write guides. Dive deeper into your topic. Create long-form blog posts that are 2,000 words or more. Not every blog post needs to be this long, but you should have some scholarly articles on your site, like white papers.

Bypass the regular online Google search engine and use Google Scholar to find current data and studies from industry publications at this website: https://scholar.google.com. You can create a profile and track articles in your library. This can help you find in-depth facts, figures, and information to aid in formulating your own long-form content.

Submit to Online Directories

Submit to 100+ Online Directories that have a high page rank by visiting this article: https://rapidboostmarketing.com/30-free-directory-submission-sites-to-drive-crazy-traffic-to-your-website. You can use this "off-page SEO tactic" of submitting your site link to online directories to improve your rank. This can generate backlinks for your blog or website and create domain authority that Google is looking for. I used this directory. I would say that approximately 80 percent of the links were valid.

It's worth it for you to check the links and submit your site. It took me a few hours to submit to these directories, but I started seeing results within 1-2 weeks of increased ranking.

This is different than submitting your site to search engines which is also a good idea—and can usually be submitted to multiple search engines at once.

Fix Broken or Dead Links

Broken or dead links are a signal to search engines that your website is not maintained and that it would not provide valuable information to readers. This can hurt your online ranking. I use the following link checker at this website:

https://www.brokenlinkcheck.com. You can enhance the user experience by providing only valid external links in your articles and also improve ranking on SERP at the same time.

The first time I used this tool, it checked through 2,307 pages and found 43 broken links. That's actually very good. Some sites have a lot more broken or dead links. I removed those broken links since they can stop search engines from crawling and indexing my site. After completing this process, which also took a few hours, I started seeing results of increased ranking within 1-2 weeks.

Check Domain Authority

Now, sites like Amazon and Alexa will have a high domain authority. However, even though you're just starting out, it's good to check the domain authority of your blog or website to see where it's at now and how far you need to go to improve it.

Use the following website to check: https://websiteseochecker.com/domain-authority-checker. When I first started doing SEO for my website and blog, the domain had a site authority of 16. It has steadily increased in the ensuing weeks. The average blog with its domain name has a DA of 30-40. Doman authority can range from 1 – 100.

Analyze Headlines for Strength

Having a strong headline that is dynamic and quickly grabs the reader's attention will improve the click-through-rate (CTR) when you promote the article online.

Use this free headline analyzer from CoSchedule: https://coschedule.com/headline-analyzer. Basically, you enter the headline and click the "analyze now" button. The first time using this tool, you will have to enter some information about your site and your goals for it. However, that's not a big deal—especially since this online tool is free.

In conclusion

Well, you've made it to the end of this **Blogger Mentoring & SEO Strategies** guide. I hope you found all this information valuable and that it's been an asset to the growth of your blog or website—and will continue to be an invaluable resource for you in the future.

Made in the USA
Monee, IL
04 November 2026

67387890R00036